HOW TO DATE SUCCESSFULLY

Susan Su

Copyright © 2023 *Susan Su*

All Rights Reserved

CONTENTS

PREFACE   **4**

DISCLAIMER   **5**

1   **What is date successfully?**   **6**

2   **What is love?**   **9**

3   **What is "falling in love"?**   **12**

4   **What means "in love with you"?**   **15**

5   **The impact of "being in love"**   **18**

6   **What is the difference between "in love" and "love"?**   **21**

7   **Love yourself first**   **24**

8	To find the one-the compatibility factor	28
8		
9	How to succeed	31
10	How to build the relationship	39
11	Five stages of relationship	42
12	Signs of a success in dating	44
13	Signs of the relationship in right track	50
14	Signs for a committed relationship	58
15	How to know if you find the one	60
16	Characteristics of a healthy relationship	62
17	What destroys a good relationship	65
18	Red flags in relationship	68
19	Signs of falling out of love	77
20	Signs of a toxic relationship	79
21	How to leave a toxic relationship?	88
22	When the relationship isn't going well	90
23	How to maintain a healthy and happy relationship?	97
24	Successful dating for marriage	102

PREFACE

Everyone dates somehow in the youth. Some people met their life partners at an early stage and their relationships are still going strong. Some have to experience and endure so many mistakes that have most likely marred the relationship and have to date again. How to date successfully is a topic for all ages.

It isn't very difficult to go out or have sex but to maintain and stay in a healthy relationship is not an easy thing. The hard thing is for two people to develop mutual trust, love and to have a meaningful enduring relationship. How to date successfully become important in order to have a mature love relationship.

Date successfully is not only about sex. This book covers topics from what is love and falling in love, what dating successfully means to various stages of dating, the challenges in each stage and how to handle them, how to know the one for you, how to date successfully, and how to maintain a healthy and happy relationship.

DISCLAIMER

The author and publisher make no representation or warranties with respect to the accuracy, applicability, fitness, or completeness of the contents of this Book; and assumes no responsibility for errors, omissions, or contrary interpretation of the subject matter herein. The author and publisher also do not warrant the performance, effectiveness or applicability of any sites listed or linked to in this Book. All links are for information purposes only and are not warranted for content, accuracy or any other implied or explicit purpose.

In practical advice books, like anything else in life, there are no guarantees of results made. Readers are cautioned to reply on their own judgment about their individual circumstances to act accordingly.

This book is not intended for use as a source of legal, psychological or counseling advice. All readers are advised to seek services of competent professionals in legal, business, accounting, and finance field.

1. WHAT IS DATING SUCESSFULLY

"Dating should be less about matching outward circumstances than meeting your inner necessity." – Mark Amend

People date for all sorts of reasons—for sex or hookups, to have a good time, to meet new people, to find someone a companion to spend time with. And there are a myriad of variables that can influence this reason for certain individuals. Of course, one of the most common reasons someone decides to date is to find a life partner, no matter the stage of life they are in.

Dating successfully can mean different things to different people, but generally, it involves building a healthy and happy romantic relationship with someone you fall in love with. Most people dating genuinely look for a serious relationship leading to lifetime partner; only some players date for fun or other reasons. So in this book, we refer "dating successfully" as forming positive and fulfilling romantic relationships that meet your needs and desires.

The earliest usage of the noun "date" is in 1896 by George Ade, a columnist for the Chicago Record. Date referred to "public" courtship, when a woman would meet a man publicly rather than privately at a residence or at court. In Ade's 1899 "Fabels in Slang", he used the term "Date Book" to describe a type of ledger system a cashier used to track dates with suitors until she married.

While the term dating has many meanings, the most common refers to a trial period in which two people explore whether to take the relationship further towards a more permanent relationship; in this sense, dating refers to the time when people are physically together in public as opposed to the earlier time period in which people are arranging the date, perhaps by corresponding by email or text or phone. Another meaning of the term dating is to describe a stage in a person's life when he or she is actively pursuing romantic relationships with different people.

Some people describe dating as two people in an intimate relationship, be it sexual, casual, long-term, short-term. Dating is the sequence that occurs before both individuals decide to be in a committed relationship, and needs to be maintained and furnished before anything stable, healthy relationship can occur. According to Cambridge Dictionary, dating means to regularly spend time with someone you have a romantic relationship with. Dating is a stage of romantic relationships in which two individuals engage in an activity together, most often with the intention of evaluating each other's suitability as a partner in a future intimate relationship.

One of the main purposes of dating is for two or more people to evaluate one another's suitability as a long term companion or spouse. Often physical characteristics, personality, financial status, and other aspects of the involved persons are judged and, as a result, feelings can be hurt and confidence shaken. Because of the uncertainty of the whole situation, the desire to be acceptable to the other person, and the possibility of rejection, dating can be very stressful for all parties involved.

So dating successfully means to build a health relationship with a romantic partner whom you love. A healthy relationship involves honesty, trust, respect and open communication between partners and they take effort and compromise from both people. There is no imbalance of power. Partners respect each other's independence, can make their own decisions without fear of retribution or retaliation, and share decisions.

2. WHAT IS LOVE

Love is composed of a single soul inhabiting two bodies."
—Aristotle

Dictionary of English defines Love as "a profoundly tender, passionate affection for another person", "a feeling of warm personal attachment or deep affection, as for a parent, child, or friend", or "sexual passion or desire". Cambridge dictionary defined it as liking another adult very much and being romantically and sexually attracted to them or having strong feelings of liking a friend or person in your family.

In 1 Corinthians 13:4–8a (ESV), Bible defined "Love is patient and kind; love does not envy or boast; it is not arrogant or rude. It does not insist on its own way; it is not irritable or resentful; it does not rejoice at wrongdoing, but rejoices with the truth." In John 15:12; John 13:34–35; Moroni 7:46–48), Jesus also told His disciples, "This is my commandment, That ye love one another, as I have loved you" for God is love (1 John 4:8).

Love is an energy, and the source is from above, God, Himself. We love God, and we have the love and received this energy from Him, then we are capable of love the world and love one another. According to Corinthians 13:1-13, Biblical love have three types: (1) Eros refers to physical or sexual love; (2) Philos means warm affection or friendship; (3) Agapē is the sacrificial, unconditional love of God.

In Greek philosophy, there are the 7 different kinds of love:

(1) Eros –passionate love, marital love--romantic love we feel with a partner who we wish to marry or have already married;

(2) Philia – affectionate, friendly love, brotherly love, love for those we hold as dear as family, not necessary by blood.

(3) Storge – unconditional, familial love, type of love we share with our family – parents, grandparents, siblings, cousins, etc.

(4) Agape – selfless and universal Love.

(5) Ludus – playful, flirtatious Love, also called young love.

(6) Pragma – committed, long-lasting Love, deep, true love that people in long, meaningful relationships experience.

(7) Philautia – self Love, appreciation and care for yourself.

So the love in dating restricts to the energy between a man and woman, mainly refer to the Eros love, "romantic, passionate love" or "physical and sexual love". It is an intense, deep affection for another person. Love can also refer to a strong feeling of this intense affection for someone, liking someone a lot. It is a combination of attraction and closeness involving emotions and behaviors characterized by passion, intimacy, and commitment. It is an emotion that keeps people bonded and committed to one another. It is caring, compassion, patience, not being jealous, not having expectations, giving yourself and other people a chance, and not rushing.

3. WHAT IS "FALLING IN LOVE"?

*"Falling in love is like getting hit by a truck and yet not being mortally wounded. just sick to your stomach, high one minute, low the next. Starving hungry but unable to eat. hot, cold, forever horny, full of hope and enthusiasm, with momentary depressions that wipe you out. It is also not being able to remove the smile from your face, loving life with a mad passionate intensity, and feeling ten years younger. – **Jackie Collins***

Dictionary of English defines "fall in love" as "to begin to feel romantic love for someone". The moment when we pass from a state of being friends with a person to loving him in a romantic way is when we fall in love. When we fall in love, we're suddenly, powerfully attracted to someone, ignoring all other attractive people.

People who experience the feeling of "falling in love" describe that it feels like "fire burning in the heart". Typically, it is how one feel when one meets another who physically, emotionally and intelligently match--it is a convincing of the heart with desire. The process, like the physical act of falling, is sudden, uncontrollable and leaves the lover in a vulnerable state, similar to "fall ill" or "fall into a trap". Sometime, one may feel like sick--having a fever. Factors known to contribute strongly to falling in love include proximity, similarity, reciprocity, and physical attractiveness.

After the fire moment, it is a forever long of the heart to be with the other person. After we fall in love, we want to share our world with that special person and constantly crave them. They are always in our mind, and become so special, and a priority. We turn to think all positive and rosy side of that person, and even find his/her quirks attractive. We see our partner as flawless, possessing infinite charm, charisma, and smarts. We care about their happiness, as much as our own. Empathy and compassion for our partner rises as we fall in love. Their traits become ours--two become one.

Love can contribute to an increased sense of well-being and lead to a positive outlook. Falling in love may make us feel like a wide-eyed, wild-hearted teenager. We generally feel more positive and hopeful. Thinking of that special person makes you smile. We feel love everywhere.

Two chemical reactions associated with falling in love are increases in oxytocin and vasopressin. Sometimes, people refer it to having chemistry. When we fall in love, we are falling into a stream of naturally occurring amphetamines running through the emotional centers of our very own brains. Our body then produces a cocktail of chemicals, including dopamine (for wanting more), noradrenaline (for excitement, focus, and attention), testosterone (for sexual interest and drive), and a drop in serotonin (which can cause that low-key obsessive feeling). These chemicals make us feel happy, giddy, energetic, euphoric, and youthful. We also feel good about ourselves and feel that we can do more. So "love is something we feel and, when we do, we say, 'This is it.'"

Studies also show that men subconsciously seek slenderness and sexiness whereas women seek status, permanence, and affluence before they seek physical attractiveness. Studies also show when comparing men who have fallen in love, their testosterone level is much higher than those that have been in a long-lasting relationship. In addition, men tend to show their emotions through actions while women tend to express their feelings with words.

4. WHAT MEANS "IN LOVE WITH YOU"

"First best is falling in love. Second best is being in love. Least best is falling out of love. But any of it is better than never having been in love." **— Maya Angelou**

Collins English Dictionary defines "be in love" as --"if you are in love with someone, you feel romantically or sexually attracted to them, and they are very important to you". So after we fall in love with someone, we are in love with that person. It generally refers to those intense feelings of infatuation and happiness that take over at the start of a relationship.

We feel that "butterflies" in our stomach, feelings of excitement and exhilaration. We also feel invincible, omnipotent, and daring. Everything feels exciting and new. We feel adventurous and full of adventures dating ideas. We have copious amounts of energy. We're intensely curious and study our beloved's every move, gesture, and word with steadfast interest, keen to know everything about this fascinating, one-of-a-kind creature; and want to learn more about each other by having shared experiences. We are very attuned to our partner's needs. When they feel sad, we feel sad. When they feel happy, we feel happy.

Being in love is a somewhat scientific process. Falling in love involves a lot of hormones, which can supercharge your feelings and make them wildly fluctuate. When we are falling in love, the increased dopamine levels in our brains drives us to concentrate on the source of our pleasure: our date. When you're around the person you love, increases in dopamine and norepinephrine lead to feelings of: pleasure, giddiness, nervous excitement, euphoria. Decreases in serotonin can fuel feelings of infatuation. Simply thinking about the object of your affections is enough to trigger dopamine release, making you feel excited and eager to do whatever it takes to see them. Then, when you actually do see them, your brain "rewards" you with more dopamine, which you experience as intense pleasure.

We also can function on a deficit of food and sleep without feeling cranky. Our rise to superhuman status is due to elevated levels of testosterone, dopamine, and epinephrine. Sex hormones, such as testosterone and estrogen, also play a part by boosting libido and leading to feelings of lust. While testosterone and dopamine create an arousal spike and lower inhibition, we are willing to have sex nearly anytime and anywhere. Sex also feel much better when you are in love, it is to make love. Dopamine activates the reward circuit, helping to make love a pleasurable experience. Physical closeness causes a burst of the bonding hormone oxytocin into our system that help us bond. We are more drawn to kissing, hugging, and touching. These key hormones, such as oxytocin and vasopressin, help cement your attraction by promoting trust, empathy, and other factors of long-term attachment.

Love has the transcendent power to lift us up where we belong, to set things straight. Everything feels exciting and new. We see the future is bright and full of potential. Oxytocin and the 'love drug' phenylalanine also make us more open and connected with others. We give spare change to buskers, smile at strangers, and bear no grudges. We become a bigger and better version of ourselves: more open, trusting, loving, generous, kind, present, patient, and forgiving.

Long-lasting love gives a feeling of having a solid ground, a safe space where you can share your inner self and be vulnerable with your feelings. It is driven by the release of hormones vasopressin and oxytocin.

5. THE IMPACT OF 'BEING IN LOVE"

"Falling in love. Being in love. It's something I dream of, something I want to feel." – Jazz Jennings

Love is a powerful emotion and can do a number on you. It can have both positive and negative impact on our well-being, body, and mind range from physical, emotional, and even psychological.

Feeling good and wonderful when you are with the person you love makes it more likely you'll keep doing it. The feelings of unconditional love, non-judgment, independence, and security that come with a healthy relationship can boost self-esteem and confidence. It also reduces stress. thoughts of your loved one can improve your mood, and maybe even provide comfort or strength when you don't feel well.

Some of the positive impacts of love in our body include reduced risk of heart diseases; less fatality risk due to heart attacks; healthy habits; increased chances of a long and healthy life; lower stress levels; reduced risk of mental health issues like depression; lower blood pressure; improved immune health; faster recovery from illness. Love that develops into a committed relationship, can have a positive impact on overall health. A loving relationship could help you have a longer life. High marital satisfaction increased this rate further. People who reported being highly satisfied in their marriage were 3.2 times more likely to be still living than those who were less satisfied.

On the other hand, the negative impact of love is also profound. Rapidly changing hormone levels can certainly affect your appetite and ability to sleep--tossing and turning in bed in agony because you can't get your love out of your mind. You may have poor judgement, doing something silly to impress someone you love.

Lovesick, lovelorn, heartbroken: these words only go to show that love doesn't always feel amazing. Love can make you miserable when your feelings go unrequited. Bad relationships that are toxic from the beginning or turn toxic with time can lead to insecurities, anxiety and stress that affect a person's mental health and future relationships. Unhealthy, unrequited love and bad relationships can negatively impact your body, mind, and well-being. These negative impacts of love can be: increased risk of heart diseases; spiked risk of heart attacks; high levels of stress; slower disease recovery; poor mental health. When you are under stress, your body responds to the stress of love by producing norepinephrine and adrenaline, the same hormones your body releases when you face danger or other crises.

The feelings of not being good enough, not doing things right, and being unable to meet expectations can make one feel less of themselves. People leaving without explanations, cheating, and lying can lead to abandonment issues that last longer than the relationship. An awareness of love's less-than-positive effects can make it easier to keep an eye out for them so they don't cause you any harm.

Love can also spark jealousy if you have a strong commitment to your partner and don't want to lose them. When you notice jealous feelings, first remind yourself they're normal. Then, share them with your partner instead of snooping or making passive-aggressive remarks about their behavior. Jealousy can actually have a positive impact on your relationship by promoting bonding and attachment — as long as you use it wisely.

6. WHAT IS THE DIFFERENCE BETWEEN "IN LOVE" AND "LOVE"

"True love is finding your soulmate in your best friend."
– Faye Hall

What is the difference between "I am in love with you "and "I love you"? So how to determine if you're in love or simply feeling love for them?

From the word meaning, being in love seems focusing more on how your partner makes you feel while loving someone involves going out of your way to make your partner's day special and to make them happy. Besides that, being in love seems that you need someone to stay happy. On the other hand, when you love, you don't only want them in your life, but also you need this person to live happily.

Being "in love" often means yearning for someone: you think about them constantly, and you crave spending time with them when you're apart. It typically refers to the excitement and wonder of early love, of mutual discovery, of delighting in fantasies, and anticipating sharing so much in the years ahead.

Intense adoration can become indifferent as time passes, and your partner's novelty can wear off. After the fantasies and illusions begin to fall away, a realistic, sustainable love may occur. Growing to love the real person and accepting who they are, with both strengths and weaknesses, can make the relationship a lasting source of comfort, emotional safety, and a wonderfully sustainable joy. Loving someone is long-lasting. Even if the person you love aggravates or disappoints you, you'll continue to care about them on some level.

In the beginning, you can be in love but not know each other well enough to overcome obstacles together. When we're in love, we tend to be on our best behavior and expect our loved one to do the same. You may be head over heels for your partner, but as soon as real problems arise, you start to feel distant from them or question their ability to outlast hard times. The connection may not be strong enough to make it through challenges unfazed.

As you relax into the relationship and accept each other realistically, there is a greater chance that those times when you aren't so witty, when you're a little cranky, or when you disagree will not be deal-breakers. When we see each other realistically and come to know each other well, we're less likely to disappoint each other. When you feel a deeper love for your long-term partner, the passion can continue to burn through life's challenges without flickering or fading away.

Love is based on the trust, respect, and honesty that develop over time. When you love someone, your relationship is strong enough to overcome life's challenges. This is because your bond with one another is so inherent that problems can actually bring you closer together. In relationships that harbor the potential of true love, people almost immediately feel the desire to confess and share everything about themselves, whether negative or positive. They feel immediately courageous, wanting to know and be known, no matter what the outcome.

When you're in love with your partner, you can develop a deeper sense of love over time as you both commit to the relationship. Being in love with someone actually sets the stage for building long-lasting love. Each partner makes appropriate sacrifices to meet the other's needs, and they'll enjoy aspects of each other that bring out the best versions of themselves. When partners enjoy spending time together, they're more motivated to grow together, take risks, and make each other's lives better.

7. LOVE YOURSELF FIRST

"To fall in love with yourself is the first secret to happiness."

– Robert Morely

Before we dive into developing a loving relationship with someone, you shall love yourself first. It's the beginning of everything. Only you love yourself first, you can become capable of loving others. The success of your relationship with others is dependent on the love you have for yourself. You cannot give to others what you do not have or own. "Love thy neighbor as thyself". In other words, the extent to which you can love others can only go as far as the depth of love you have for yourself. To have a successful loving relationship, start by loving yourself.

Self-love means having a high regard for your own well-being and happiness. Self-love means taking care of your own needs and not sacrificing your well-being to please others. Self-love means not settling for less than you deserve. When you love yourself you have compassion for yourself. You accept your own weaknesses, appreciate these so-called shortcomings as something that makes you who you are. Self-love helps us take care of ourselves, lower stress, and strive for success.

Life responds to us proportionately to the depth of our self-awareness and self-esteem, and also to the clarity of our individual or personal self-image. Self-love, then, is the ultimate activating code to unlocking our power and Godhood. It facilitates the alignment of our mental, emotional and psychical faculties for optimal expression. With self-love, we express true humanity, one that is graceful, beautiful and divine. Self-love creates a powerful and magnetic force field that attracts all the experiences we need as individuals for our evolutionary journeys. True self-love is the foundation of real alchemy, your path to everything. You desire is directly proportionate to the depth of love you have for yourself.

Self-love is important because it motivates much of our positive behavior while reducing harmful behavior. It both empowers us to take risks and to say no to things that don't work for us. It's a key component of building self-compassion. How you love yourself is how you teach others to love you.

Self-love is simply unconditional affectionate regard for oneself. It is looking at oneself the way God sees one, with pure love.

Self-love is knowing without question that you are worthy and ever validated. Self-Love is knowing that you are already everything you are looking for. The foundation of a healthy and strong self-awareness, self-esteem, self-confidence, and self-image is contingent upon unconditional self-love. You will be kind to others if you are kind to yourself. You will be able to love others if you love yourself.

Love and appreciate yourself. Forget about the terrible past and move on. Accept and forgive yourself, and be grateful for your life. Loving yourself should always be a top priority, including self-acceptance, self-compassion, self-care. More specific, accept yourself just as you are, accept your mistakes and flaws, don't compare yourself to others, establish boundaries (Love yourself enough to set boundaries. Your time and energy are precious. You get to choose how you use it. You teach people how to treat you by deciding what you will and won't accept), and perform activities that make you happy--spending time performing your interest-- one of the easiest things to love yourself because your passion makes you feel good about yourself. Love yourself first and everything else falls into line. You really have to love yourself to get anything done in this world.

Self-love is not the same as narcissism. Narcissism is extreme self-involvement to the degree that it makes a person ignore the needs of those around them. While everyone may show occasional narcissistic behavior, true narcissists frequently disregard others or their feelings. They also do not understand the effect that their behavior has on other people. True self-love is not asking to love yourself more than those around you. No. Rather, it is asking you to love yourself FIRST, then you are FULLY equipped to love and relate well with others. Remember, you can only give what you have or own, and not what you don't have.

8. TO FIND THE ONE-- THE COMPATIBILITY FACTOR

"You meet thousands of people and none of them really touch you. And then you meet one person and your life is changed forever." – Love & Other Drugs

Compatibility refers to the ability of two people to coexist peacefully and harmoniously, while also supporting and fulfilling each other's needs. Compatibility encompasses many different aspects of a relationship, including physical attraction, emotional connection, shared interests and values, communication style, and lifestyle choices. With so many different personalities, values, and lifestyles out there, by identifying the qualities you're looking for in a partner, you can increase your chances of finding someone who is truly compatible with you, thereby making dating a success.

Compatibility is one of the most important factors to consider when it comes to dating and relationships. It is the foundation upon which any successful and long-lasting relationship is built. In simple terms, compatibility refers to the degree to which two people are able to coexist and thrive together in a romantic relationship. These factors play a crucial role not only in determining whether two people are truly compatible and able to form a lasting bond, but also if "love fire" can generate in between the two people, in another word, weather the two individuals will be able to fall in love or not. When you meet someone who physically, intelligent and emotionally compatible with you, you find the one--the one for you.

Physical attraction is often the first thing that draws people to one another. However, it is important to note that physical attraction alone is not enough to sustain a relationship over time. Emotional connection is equally important, and involves a deeper understanding and appreciation of one another's thoughts, feelings, and emotions.

Shared interests and values are important in determining compatibility. When two people have similar hobbies, passions, and beliefs, they are more likely to have a strong connection and be able to enjoy each other's company. This shared sense of purpose can also help to build a strong foundation for the relationship, as both partners are working towards common goals.

Communication style is another important aspect of compatibility. Effective communication is key to any successful relationship, and partners who are able to communicate openly and honestly with one another are more likely to form a deep and lasting bond. It is important for both partners to be able to listen to one another and express their thoughts and feelings in a respectful and understanding manner.

Finally, lifestyle choices are also an important factor in determining compatibility. When two people have similar lifestyles, such as similar work schedules or hobbies, they are more likely to be able to spend time together and enjoy each other's company. This can also help to reduce conflict and tension within the relationship, as both partners are able to enjoy their time together without feeling pressured or stressed.

9. HOW TO SUCCEED THE FIRST-DATE

Love is so unpredictable. Sometimes you'll know a man for years and then one day, boom! Suddenly you see him in a different way. And other times, it's that first date, that first moment. That's what makes it so great – Sarah Dessen

First date is all about knowing each other better and to see if you can be together in a relationship. It doesn't matter that you have to go for a coffee, date, a dinner date, or a lunch date, or hiking as the first date. The real thing for the first date is to see each other and get to know each other to see that if both of you want to build a relationship, at the same time, to build your emotional connection for the next date and to further establish a relationship. So it is important that look and feel however you feel most confident and comfortable.

What most important at the first date is communication -- how to communicate beyond the words. Psychic communication is part of that invisible, rarely-understood "hidden" world. Through psychic communication, you will get the desired results of what you want with your interactions and relationships. You can send, receive, and maybe even implant messages into other people's minds while you're in a state called "alpha state" of consciousness - a state that is ideal for tapping into some of your very powerful mental powers. Being in the alpha allows you to communicate with others and to send positive energy of what you want on a different level, on a more powerful level, without using words. It is all in your brain and mind--that is to communicate, influence, and attract.

In that state, you basically tap into the power of the God, the universe. You are in harmony with yourself, also radiant a positive energy- an emotion of love, confidence and magnetic power and love. As a happy person, you will draw other happy, fun people to you and will also infect other people's energy with your own. And "love" is the most fundamental, the rawest form, and the most universally-understood representation of attraction, seduction and magnetism. In a sense, if you want your partner to fall in love with you, the mind will reveal you the steps to achieve that, and also attracts the right energy and resources to you to help you achieve that.

Body language is another vital part of human communication. Even minor details about your emotions are revealed through your body language. Your every move is crucial here. Successful people try to maintain positive body language. Make sure that you create moves in a positive way and look attractive. For an example, when you are at a Starbucks coffee, make sure that you sit comfortably there. Keep your legs and shoulders relaxed and pretend as if you own the place and are a regular there.

Don't strain your voice or speak too fast, it will just make you seem nervous and jittery. Try and attain a sexy and sensuous voice. Suppose he shops at a particular grocery store; mention that you were there at the same time, possibly while he was shopping there. Then add punch lines like "How could I miss such an amazing man!". This type of conversation and comments make you both feel as if you have known each other for ages. Let the conversation progresses and remind him about many other coincidences. These conversations will make him feel closer to you. As the guy thinks about all these conversations, he will consider that fate meant for you to be together. And at a deeper psychic level, he will conclude that you are the woman that he had been waiting for all his life.

It is also important to get you partner to relax around you, it means making him comfortable enough so that he feels that you are not pressuring him into getting into a serious relationship with you until he wants it. For example, imagine that you are at the coffee where you met and in mid- conversation with the man. In the middle of the conversation ask him to stay still and close his eyes. Just behave as if there is still sleep in his eye and pretend that you brushed it off. Once you two finish your meal and leave the restaurant, ask him to hold still again. With your finger again brush off an imaginary hair from his lower lip. The benefits of this technique include sub-communicating the fact that you two are very comfortable around each other. It also involves you touching his face. Most men have erogenous zones on their lower lip and this has a high focus of nerve endings. A light touch here would stimulate his lower lip and make his body liberate sex hormones, and create a feeling similar to the feeling of falling in love. When you put a man at ease, he just knows it feels good to be with you and it feels right. You want to make you partner feel so good around you that he/she will want to be with you all the time. He will miss you when you are not around, and he will want to be with you for the rest of his life because it feels good for him; and being with you feels better than being without you. Er

Last, remember, of all the first dates people can go on, the most popular among now-married couples are the simplest. The less complicated the interaction is, the more likely it is for a potential partnership to emerge because you're not distracted, leaving you more able to focus on the other person, how you feel around them, and whether an attraction is building.

10. HOW TO BUILD THE RELATIONSHIP

"However successful you are, there is no substitute for a close relationship. We all need them." — Francesca Annis

A successful relationship requires work and effort from both individuals. You both have to be willing to give your all to make the relationship work. Here are some key strategies to make your relationship grow stronger.

(1) **Focus on the present, not the past:** Once you are in a relationship, that is not the best time to bring your past fears and experiences; whether good or bad to the surface. Your strength and effort should be on your partner now. You don't have to focus on the past in your present relationship. There will be time later if the person is the one for you and you are both willing to make it work to bring out the skeletons in the cupboard; not on the first date.

(2) **Make sure you're attracted to the person and not the idea of the relationship**: Dating fatigue is real, and sometimes we want a relationship so strongly that we don't even recognize we're more drawn to the idea of a relationship than the person we're with. You run the risk of forcing a spark or putting other people into boxes they

don't belong in (or don't want to be in) if you're so focused on finding Happily Ever After.

(3) **Meet each other's friends**: Meeting your partner's friends tell you what kind of person they are.

(4) **Be yourself**: You have to be yourself from the start of the relationship. Don't hide your flaws and strengths.

(5) **Don't worry about labels**: There is no reason to label your relationship, it's your relationship and if you're not ready for that yet, don't feel pressured and label it. Besides, you don't have anything to prove to anybody. The relationship is yours.

(6) **Stop bringing up your ex**: Bringing up your ex when you're sad or happy or overwhelmed is doing nothing but carefully removing the foundation you are laying together, and the house will not stay on a poorly built foundation. No one wants to feel like they are being measured against someone else and it also doesn't help to compare your past relationships to your present relationship. Focus on the present, your past is over.

(7) **Relationships are not 50/50 but 100/100:** Contrary to popular misconception, you can't just contribute what you think is your share. Relationships really aren't all about compromise or trying

for 50/50. For a happy, successful, long-lasting relationship, give all that you're capable of and expect the same in return. Of course, conflicts will arise, but you both should be 100% in the relationship. You have to be willing to both give your all to the relationship.

(8) **Communication is key**: You have to be willing to communicate how you feel at all times. You can't expect your partner to read your mind.

(9**) Actions will always matter more than words ever will**: It's not enough to announce your love ten times a day or scream it out from the mountaintop. If you don't act like it, the relationship is doomed. It doesn't matter if they're promising to take you on vacation or that they want to introduce you to their parents if they're not making consistent plans, making you feel special, and showing you how they feel about you (instead of just telling you).

(10**) Spend quality time together**. Quality time is all about mindfully spending time together in order to show your appreciation & affection for one another, and increase connection and intimacy in your relationship. It is also a great way to build our friendship. It gives us shared interests as well as the opportunity to have fun and laugh together.

11. FIVE STAGES OF RELATIONSHIP

"Dating is an emotional experience. You're vulnerable. You're letting someone you barely know see the real you." — Joy Browne

From first date to a committed relationship, there are five stage of relationship. Though these stages are sometimes referred to by different names, the concept of the five relationship stages is recognized by relationship experts far and wide. These are the romance stage, the power struggle stage, the stability stage, the commitment stage, the co-creation or bliss stage. By understanding the 5 stages of a relationship, you'll expect each stage and not get "stuck" in any of them.

(1) Attraction and Romance Stage:

The Romance Stage begins when we fall in love with someone. It is also called the honeymoon phase. In this stage, we experience love in its most immature form – infatuation. This is where we have that initial attraction, the urge to get to know each other and move things on to something more serious. Our brains release a cocktail of hormones that help maintain the attraction such as dopamine, oxytocin, etc. We feel that all-consuming love, joy and can be fueled by passionate sex. We can only see what we have in common or similar, and all of our partner's good qualities. This is the stage at which everything feels very new and exciting and seems almost perfect.

(2) Crisis Stage:

After the romance stage grinds to a halt when your brain stops producing those love chemicals, the relationship arrives at the crisis stage, also called the power struggle stage. The rose colored glasses are off now. Feelings of disappointment and anger replace it. Instead of only seeing the similarities (as you did in the Romance stage), now all you can see are differences and flaws.

Often one partner withdraws, shutting down their heart and pulling away to get some space…while the other partner pursues them, demanding their attention while feeling desperately afraid that they are being emotionally deserted. Challenges actually bring couples who manage them correctly closer through the tough times together and trust each other through communication.

The power struggles between the couple and disappointments can escalate. We may want to fight for our values, needs and wants to be met and this can in some cases translate into a need to be right all the time. This stage can last anywhere from a few months to many years. How long it lasts for you two will depend on your willingness to embrace change, childhood history, and the quality of the relationship repair advice you receive.

There are 2 ways most couples deal with their Power Struggle stage. (a) BREAK UP: They take the nearest exit and break up. The relationship gets dissolved. You might find that these are the 'almost' relationships with people who end up being a friend or acquaintance down the road. (b) SURVIVE: They continue along their journey together, surviving through the pain and frustration of a relationship. People who have chosen this option typically think that good relationships involve sacrifice and compromise. Their relationship eventually emotionally flat-lines, along with their sex life.

The third option is to get past your Power Struggle. You graduate from the Power Struggle stage when you:

- discover a reliable way to communicate kindly about emotionally charged topics,

- can quickly repair emotional disconnections between you,

- can heal old hurt and restore broken trust,

- learn to share power,

- give up your fantasies of harmony without struggle, and

- accept and appreciate each other's differences.

(3) Working Stage:

Once you've learned how to fight in a way that both of you win, you move to the working relationship stage. A period of relative peace follows, also called "the stable stage".

It finally becomes very clear that you're never ever going to succeed in changing your partner and you've given up trying to. You're OK with your partner being different from you. You both have clear boundaries and you need to learn mutual respect. You've actually resolved your differences and gotten on the same page together, the thrill of being loved returns, and in a deeper, more mature form than in the Romance stage.

(4) Commitment Stage:

Once you get past the working stage, you enter the commitment stage. In this stage, you fully surrender to the reality that you and your partner are human and that your relationship has shortcomings as a result. You choose each other consciously. You begin to experience a beautiful balance of love, belonging, fun, power, and freedom.

You express a desire to be with each other exclusively and you have grown to not only recognize but accept the flaws that may come with your partner. You begin learning about each other's pasts and deeper feelings and seeing their true character in a new light. You are realizing that what you have is deeper than "fun, exciting, and sexy" It is a bond and trust that keeps you together.

5. **Real Love/Bliss Stage:**

This is the stage where you realize you two are best friends, lovers and partners in life—and you only better each other and feel as though you are one unit. In this stage, couples are finding a deeper connection with each other and a balanced life. They have been through the previous stages and are more accepting of each other and themselves. They are often more relaxed and the passion has been reignited between them. They are more likely to use effective communication with one another than the previous attacking/defending stance. They've learned to love their partner regardless of the mess or flaws they have. They remember the great times fondly and the bad times make they realize it was all worth it after all. This is the stage when the next step is taken; moving in with each other, having kids, getting married.

12. SIGNS OF A SUCCESS IN DATING

"Throughout life you will meet one person who is unlike any other. This person is one you could forever talk to. They understand you in a way that no one else does or even could. This person is your soul mate, your best friend. Don't ever let them go, for they're your guardian angel sent from heaven above"— Pamela Ann,

For a successful dating, there are makers that you shall see in your partner and your relationship. These signs are the must-have for a good relationship and if you don't have, develop them.

(1) COMMUNICATION: Successful dating involves open, honest and effective communication between partners. This means being able to express your thoughts, feelings, and boundaries clearly and listening attentively to your partner's perspective. To communicate effectively, make sure to: **(a)** be precise and clear; (b) listening attentively: show that you're interested in what they have to say by paying attention and asking questions; (c) Communicate with body language, facial expressions, and voice tone; (d) be respectful: avoid criticizing or insulting the partners; (e) offer constructive criticism and effective feedback.

(2) COMPATIBILITY: compatibility--means sharing values, interests. Factors to consider for assessing compatibility include: shared values and beliefs about important issues like family, religion, politics, and personal goals; common interest in hobbies, sports, or entertainment; healthy and effective communication styles; similar emotional need and mutual support, and similar lifestyle such as work schedules, living arrangements, and financial goals.

(3) RESPECT: it means treating each other with kindness, empathy, and consideration, and valuing each other's time and energy, paying attention to cach other's feelings, listening to one another's thoughts and opinions, and avoiding speaking negatively about one another or acting negatively toward them. It also entails respecting each other's personal space and abstaining from abusive, domineering, or hurtful behavior. Respect also involves celebrating and embracing one another's differences. Partners in a healthy relationship are aware of each other's individuality and the fact that we all have our own views and experiences.

(4) TRUST: Trust means being reliable, honest, transparent, and maintaining boundaries. It instills a sense of safety and security in the relationship. When there is trust, partners can be themselves and feel comfortable opening up and sharing their thoughts, feelings, desire and experiences. They understand that their partners will not judge them or exploit their flaws. It strengthens the emotional bond, fosters intimacy, and enables them to rely on one another.

(5) **GROWTH:** This means being open to learning from each other, supporting each other's goals, and growing together as a couple. It includes: (a) personal Growth: Partners encourage each other to pursue their goals, try new things, and step out of their comfort zones to explore their interests, passions, and aspirations. (b) Emotional Growth: partners encourage each other to communicate openly and honestly, to express their feelings, to work through conflicts together, and support each other through challenging times. (c) Interpersonal Growth: Partners help each other develop effective communication skills, healthy boundaries, mutual respect, and learn to work collaboratively. (d) Relationship Growth: Partners continually evolve and adapt to the changing needs of each other.

(6) **AFFECTION:** Affection is a feeling of fondness, care, warmth, or love towards your partner. Learning how to show affection fosters a healthy relationship where both partners feel validated and cherished: listen to your partner; do something for

them; say that you love them; go on dates; plan a surprise for them; always make time for your partner; remember the little details; be intimate; help them; be your partner's best friend.

(7) BOTH CAN MEET AT THE MIDDLE: Both parties should be able to agree to disagree. The secret to a successful relationship is compromise: truly listen to your partner; don't always try to be right; let things go; rethink your expectations; be willing to change; keep an open mind; show appreciation; be flexible.

(8) FEEL GOOD ABOUT YOURSELF: A successful relationship should have both individuals feeling good about themselves. Here are some of the things that go a long way into making your partner feel good about themselves: notice the little thing your partner does for you; always acknowledge your partner's presence with joy; compliment something they do well; show consistent support.

(9) GREAT LISTENERS: A good partner always makes you feel heard and will listen attentively to everything you have to say. To be one, you can try to pay attention; ask questions; validate your partner's feelings; avoid judgement and criticisms; and offer support;

(10) **COMMITMENT:** Commitment refers to the intention and willingness to work through challenges, make sacrifices, and invest time and effort into maintaining a partnership. It provides a sense of security and stability and creates a foundation of mutual respect and loyalty for both partners. To build commitment, try to: make a commitment statement; give your partner consistent attention, devotion and loyalty; cherish your relationship's milestones; learn your partner's love language and express yours in those ways; consider your partner when making important decisions, such as future plan, put their needs first before your own; work through conflicts effectively.

(11) KINDNESS: Kindness creates positive feelings and builds strong relationships, increase self-esteem and happiness, and improve overall well-being. It also has a ripple effect, inspiring others to pay it forward and create a more compassionate and supportive society. To be kind, try to love your partner sincerely and genuinely; be a source of comfort; respect and appreciate each other; inspire them to be positive; offer to help when you can; be grateful.

(12) **INDIVIDUALITY:** Individuality is a reflection of our true self and is essential for a vibrant and successful dating experience. It

is important to have a strong sense of self, to be open to exploring different aspects of yourself, and be able to express yourself in a genuine and honest manner.

(13) SUPPORT EACH OTHER'S GOALS: Supporting each other's goals creates an environment of mutual respect, encouragement, community and belonging which helps build your relationship. Having a strong support system encourages trying new things, taking more risks and pursuing past recessed goals.

(14) MAKE DECISIONS TOGETHER: To grow a healthy relationship, making decisions together is key. To do that, make sure to be open to your partner's stance; examine the pros and cons together; seek genuine agreement.

(15) ACCEPTING IRRESOLVABLE AND PERPETUAL CONFLICTS: These perpetual conflicts may arise due to fundamental differences in values, beliefs, or personality traits that are unlikely to change. What matters is not solving perpetual problems, but rather the effect with which they are discussed. The goal should be to establish a dialogue about the perpetual problem that communicates acceptance of your [marriage] partner with humor, affection, and even amusement.

13. SIGNS OF THE RELATIONSHIP IN RIGHT TRACK

"Dating is like searching for the perfect wine. One date is too fruity, another too dry, and still another too much bouquet (cologne overdose). But once you find the perfect variety that suits your taste, get drunk." – Katie Kosko

Cultivating a healthy relationship is crucial. A great relationship is a safe place for both people to love, honor, and respect one another. Here are signs that your relationship is on the right track.

(1) **You're not afraid to speak up.** To speak up in a relationship means that you are willing to express your thoughts, feelings, and opinions openly and honestly with your partner. It allows both partners to have a clear understanding of each other's perspectives and feelings, which can help to build trust and empathy. It can also help to resolve conflicts and prevent misunderstandings from escalating into bigger problems. Regardless of what you are feeling at that particular point in time, you are not afraid of speaking up, even if it may be different from your partner's. This can involve discussing difficult topics, addressing issues that may be causing tension or conflict, or simply communicating your needs and desires. It requires a willingness to be vulnerable and a commitment to actively listen and understand your partner's point of view. Ultimately, being able to communicate openly and honestly help to strengthen a relationship and foster a deeper connection between partners.

(2)   **Mutual trust.** Trust is the belief that you can rely on and have confidence in your partner to be honest, faithful, and dependable. Building trust in a relationship requires consistent honesty, reliability, and follow-through on commitments. It also involves being open and transparent with your partner about your thoughts, feelings, and actions. When trust is established in a relationship, it can provide a strong foundation for the relationship to grow and thrive. Trust allows partners to feel comfortable and secure with each other, which can lead to deeper emotional intimacy and a stronger bond. Trust also enables partners to work through challenges and conflicts more effectively because they know that they can rely on each other.   Without trust, a relationship can become unstable and insecure, which can lead to tension, conflict, and ultimately, the breakdown of the relationship

(3) You Know Each Other's Love Language. Knowing your partner's love language and letting them know yours is a way to help you both feel loved and appreciated. There are five love languages and these are: words of affirmation, physical touch, quality time, acts of service, gifts giving. You can either ask your partner or observe what makes them happy and do it.

(4) You can agree to disagree on certain issues. Agree to disagree is the resolution of a conflict that requires all parties to tolerate the opposing positions, even when they do not accept it as the best choice. Disagreement does not have to lead to hostility. In fact, it can lead to discussion and better understanding of ourselves and others. Positive agreeing to disagree occurs when individuals recognize that further conflict would be unnecessary, ineffective or otherwise undesirable. While unresolved disagreements can lead to charged conflict between people, agreeing to disagree allows us to feel closer and can also lead to an increased understanding of one another because it requires us to hear the other point of view.

(5) You Encourage Each Other to Go After Your Goals. Encouraging your partner to pursue their goals involves being supportive, positive, and uplifting. It means taking an interest in your partner's dreams and aspirations, and actively helping them to achieve them in any way you can. This could involve providing emotional support, offering advice or resources, or even helping with practical tasks or logistics. When partners encourage each other to pursue their goals, it creates a sense of partnership and collaboration in the relationship. It shows that both partners are invested in each other's growth and success, and that they believe in each other's abilities. When both partners are motivated and driven to achieve their own personal goals, it can lead to a more fulfilling, satisfying, balanced and well-rounded relationship overall. It also provides new opportunities for shared experiences and learning from each other.

(6) You Are in Your Own Skin, Feel Happy and Supported.

When you are in a relationship where you are comfortable with who you are, that relationship is definitely moving forward. Feeling happy and supported can help improve communication, increased trust and foster deeper emotional connection. It means having a partner who is there for you emotionally, encourages you, respects you, and shows you affection to foster a deep sense of connection and trust, and contribute to a positive and fulfilling relationship.

(7)   You and Your Partner Hold Separate Interests. Holding separate interests is a sign that you are in a healthy relationship because it allows each partner to maintain their individuality and pursue their own passions. Having separate interests also provides opportunities for each partner to learn from the other and broaden their own horizons. It's important, however, that each partner makes an effort to support and respect the other's interests, even if they don't necessarily share them.

(8)   Boundaries Are Honored and Respected. Boundaries are the physical, emotional, and mental limits that individuals set for themselves in order to protect their well-being and maintain their sense of self. When boundaries are not honored and respected, it can lead to feelings of resentment, anger, and mistrust. It's important to have open and honest communication about boundaries from the beginning of the relationship and to continue to check in with each other regularly to ensure that those boundaries are still being respected and honored. Communicate clearly about what your boundaries are, and to listen to and respect your partner's boundaries as well. This can include respecting each other's personal space and privacy, and being open and honest about your feelings and needs.

(9)   Playfulness or lightheartedness: Being playful and lighthearted can help build a sense of intimacy and trust in a relationship, as it allows partners to let down their guard and be themselves in a more relaxed and playful way. It can also help diffuse tension, conflict when things get tough, bring joy, spontaneity, and fun into the dynamic. It allows couples to connect in a more carefree and light-hearted way, which can be a great counterbalance to the stresses of daily life. Playfulness can come in many different forms, whether it's engaging in silly activities together, making each other laugh, or teasing each other in a playful way. It can also involve being spontaneous, and not taking things too seriously all the time.

(10)   **Teamwork:** Teamwork is incredibly important in a relationship because it creates a sense of partnership and collaboration between partners. When both individuals work together towards common goals, they can achieve more than they would be able to alone. Teamwork is at the heart of great achievement. Elements of a good team are things like communication, respect, helpfulness and compromise. When partners work together, they learn to rely on each other and build trust. When partners trust each other, they can rely on each other to follow through on commitments

and support each other through challenges. When partners work as a team, they must communicate clearly and honestly to ensure that they are both on the same page. This improves communication skills and reduces misunderstandings or conflict. They aslo can share responsibilities and tasks, which reduces stress and workload for both individuals. This allows each partner to feel supported and valued in the relationship, which can improve overall satisfaction and reduce tension. When partners work together towards common goals, they create a sense of unity and togetherness. This can help partners feel closer and more connected to each other, which can strengthen the relationship over time.

(11) **Emotional intimacy:** Emotional intimacy can be expressed in verbal and non-verbal communication. The degree of comfort, effectiveness, and mutual experience of closeness might indicate emotional intimacy between individuals. When you connect deeply with your partner by expressing your feelings and sharing your vulnerabilities, you are experiencing emotional intimacy. Sharing your deepest thoughts and emotions with your partner is, for many couples, one of the most rewarding aspects of their relationship.

Emotional intimacy is simply a deeper understanding of your partner. It is being aware of all of their emotions, hopes, dreams, vulnerabilities, fears, motivations, and desires. It's getting a better understanding of what motivates or moves your spouse, what interests and intrigues, enthralls and enchants that person to whom you've committed yourself. Emotional intimacy is a never-ending process of discovering, comprehending, and empathizing with who your spouse is on the inside. Emotional connection is important to both men and women in a long-term, healthy relationship. Signs of emotional intimacy includes:

- You feel safe sharing your private issues and concerns.

- You feel supported—like someone has your back, not alone.

- You know your partner will listen to you without judgment.

- You can easily shift from light to deeper conversation.

- You are able to feel empathy for your partner.

- You are genuinely interested in your partner and welcome them sharing their feelings and experiences with you

- When your partner is suffering, your heart opens up and you feel deep compassion for them.

14. SIGNS FOR A COMMITTED RELATIONSHIP

"You always have two choices: your commitment versus your fear." — Sammy Davis, Jr.

A committed relationship is an interpersonal relationship based upon commitment to one another involving love, trust, honesty, openness. Committed people have priorities and they stick to those priorities. They are loyal to their families, their friends, their team, their sport and themselves because they are determined to succeed. Commitment also means that you promise to support your partner now and in the future. They have a more long-range view of things and make decisions based on what's best for the relationship, not what's best for themselves as individuals.

A man will commit when he feels a deep connection with a woman that he doesn't feel with anyone else; when he finds a lover who is also his best friend that makes him feel special and unique. Men feel deeply attracted to women who have the traits they appreciate and cherish, such as intelligence, sense of humor, compassion, kindness, and loyalty. If your guy is serious about the relationship, usually, he will go out of his way to make you a priority.

Signs of a man is committed: he lets his guard down; he takes you to meet his family and closest friends, he wants to be around you, he values your advice and opinions, he is your biggest cheerleader, he defends you.

Signs of a committed relationship are:

• They Portray You in a Positive Light. People in committed relationships tend to portray their partners in the best possible light; they minimize their flaws and emphasize their positive attributes.

• They Speak in "We". Someone who feels committed speaks about themselves as "we."

• They Meet Your Needs. Those who choose to be in relationships are committed because they are meeting each other's needs.

• They Are Highly Satisfied. If you feel highly satisfied, you are more likely to want to commit to a relationship.

• They Are Disinterested in Pursuing Others. People in committed relationships don't pay attention to potential alternative partners.

• They Make Sacrifices. Committed partners make sacrifices for each other and don't expect favors to be returned.

15. HOW TO KNOW IF YOU FIND THE ONE

"Throughout life you will meet one person who is unlike any other. This person is one you could forever talk to. They understand you in a way that no one else does or even could. This person is your soul mate, your best friend. Don't ever let them go, for they're your guardian angel sent from heaven above"— Pamela Ann,

We've all grown up with the fairy tale that there is a special person specially made for you, but that is not the case. In your lifetime, you will meet several people who can be potential "the ones". You'll know you've found "the one" when you feel at peace, content in your life together, wanting for nothing more.

You naturally adjust and change a little bit when you get into a relationship with someone because of the things they bring out in you; in other words, your partner has an effect on you. Everybody has different tastes and types and personalities often attract certain personalities, so how do you know "The one" for you?

- The one will be a relationship-oriented person.

- You don't feel the need to change for that person.

- You are ready to fight for the relationship.

- You can trust the person

- The One might not have everything in common with you, but he/she will respect any differences.

- The One will be someone whose flaws you're able to acknowledge—and still tolerate.

- You happily sacrifice for the one.

- They are your number one cheerleaders.

- Your body is happy.

- The One will be someone who makes you laugh at yourself.

- You've Planned Your Lives Together and You Couldn't be Happier about It.

- There is no idea of doubt in you.

16. CHARACTERISTICS OF A HEALTHY RELATIONSHIP

"A healthy relationship is one where you can't wait to see that person. You love to be around that person. You can't get enough of that person. You're at your best when you're with that person."

— Germany Kent

Love being in a relationship and think you have found the one? Trust, companionship, space and love are the characteristics of a healthy relationship! The following are several detail characteristics of a good and health relationship.

- Respect for privacy and space: It involves recognizing and honoring each other's boundaries, allowing each other to have alone time, and not intruding on each other's personal lives without permission. It simply means recognizing each other's need for independence and allowing each other to have personal time and space. By doing so, you can build a stronger and more respectful relationship based on trust and mutual understanding. You don't have to be with your partner all the time.

- Your partner encourages you to participate in activities that you enjoy. A healthy relationship involves a balance between time spent together and time spent apart. Encouraging each other to have separate interests and social lives can actually strengthen the relationship, as it allows both partners to grow as individuals and come back to the relationship with new experiences and perspectives.

- You feel physically safe, and your partner doesn't force you to have sex or to do things that make you feel uncomfortable.

- Your partner respects your wishes and feelings and you can compromise and negotiate when there are disagreements or conflicts. Respect for each other's wishes and feelings is an essential component of any successful partnership. When disagreements or conflicts arise, the ability to compromise can help to ensure that both partners' needs are met and that the relationship remains strong.

- Effective communication: Both partners should be willing to express their thoughts and feelings openly and honestly, while also actively listening to the other person's perspective.

- Conflict Resolution: It is important approach any disagreements or conflicts with a collaborative mindset, seeking solutions that work for both rather than trying to "win" the argument. Conflict can actually be an opportunity to strengthen your relationship if you handle it in a healthy and productive way. By listening to each other, expressing your own needs clearly, and working together to find solutions, you can build trust and understanding that can help to sustain your relationship over time.

- Friendship: The bedrock of the relationship, what will make it stand is friendship. You have to be friends with your partner.

- Forgiveness: You have to be willing to forgive both yourself and your partner--past mistakes, present mistakes and also prepare yourself to forgive future mistakes.

- Time: a successful relationship is only born when both individuals are willing to sacrifice their time for each other. You have to be willing to be there for that person, be willing to listen and be willing to just spend time together.

- Accountability: You have to be accountable for your mistakes and errors. You cannot expect to build a strong and stable relationship by pushing blame on each other. That only serves to make the relationship tenser than it should be.

17. WHAT DESTROYS A GOOD RELATIONSHIP

"Things can be fixed. Relationship CANNOT. It's like standing on a cracked glass plane, you might just adjust yourself for the time being but there will always be a fear of increasing the cracks, fear of falling through, fear of being destroyed. ---Hanif Hassan Barbhuiya

Relationships are fragile and often get affected by small little things if not taken care of properly. It doesn't always have to be a massive blowout that ends things; sometimes, it's many little things that could cause significant problems in relationships. Another big mistake couples tend to make is to take their relationship for granted, to take their love for granted. By doing so, they carelessly begin to erode the quality of connection with harsh words, working too much, or devoting too much time to a hobby. Love is a choice—every single day. There are so many of these possible little things that can destroy a good relationship. Mare sure not to do these.

(1) **Keeping your attention on what's wrong:** Focusing on what's wrong in your relationship can be detrimental to its health and longevity. While it's important to address issues in your relationship, constantly dwelling on them create a negative and toxic environment.

(2) Competing to get your needs met: While it's important for both partners to have their needs met, approaching the relationship with a competitive mindset can lead to a lack of cooperation and collaboration. It creates an unhealthy dynamic that ultimately undermines the well-being of both partners. It can also create a power struggle, a lack of emotional connection; lead to feelings of resentment which will in turn destroy the relationship.

(3) Withholding your love or hurting back when hurt: it is a common but damaging behavior that can quickly erode the trust and emotional intimacy in the relationship. While it's natural to feel hurt and defensive when someone you love hurts you, responding with spiteful or vengeful behavior only exacerbates the problem by creating a cycle of negative behavior, lead to feelings of resentment and damage yours and/or your partner's self-esteem.

(4) Taking your partner for granted: Taking your partner for granted in your relationship can lead to feelings of resentment and dissatisfaction. When you become complacent and stop appreciating your partner's efforts, it can create an unhealthy dynamic in the relationship that can lead to a breakdown in communication, trust, and emotional intimacy.

(5) **Holding grudges:** Holding grudges in your relationship can be toxic and damaging to the health of the relationship. When you hold on to anger and resentment, it can create a negative and hostile environment that undermines trust, communication, and emotional intimacy in the relationship.

(6) **Piling negative emotions:** Piling negative emotions in your relationship can be detrimental to the health of the relationship. When you consistently bottle up negative emotions like anger, frustration, and resentment, it can create a toxic environment that undermines trust, communication, and emotional intimacy in the relationship.

(7) **Doubting your partner:** Doubting your partner can be damaging to the trust and intimacy that are essential for a healthy relationship. When you constantly doubt your partner, it creates a negative and suspicious environment that undermines the foundation of the relationship.

(8) **Depending too much on each other:** While interdependence and mutual support are essential for a healthy relationship, depending too much on one another can create a sense of entanglement and loss of individuality that can stifle personal growth and autonomy. It suffocates the relationship in the long run.

(9) Being ignorant your appearance: Being ignorant about your appearance in a relationship can have a negative impact on the overall health of the relationship. While appearance isn't everything, taking care of yourself and making an effort to present yourself in a positive way can contribute to feelings of attraction, confidence, and self-esteem.

(10) Disrespect: Disrespect in a relationship can be extremely damaging to the health and longevity of the relationship. Disrespect can manifest in many ways, including belittling, insulting, ignoring, and dismissing one's partner.

(11) Being overly possessive: Being overly possessive in a relationship can have a negative impact on the overall health and well-being of the relationship. Possessiveness can manifest in many ways, including jealousy, controlling behavior, and a lack of trust.

(12) Not respecting each other's space: Not respecting each other's space in a relationship can be detrimental to the health of the relationship. It's important for individuals in a relationship to have their own space and time to pursue their interests, hobbies.

(13) Mistreat your partner in front of friends or family: It can be damaging to the relationship and can erode trust and emotional intimacy. It is also humiliating and embarrassing for the partner who is being mistreated.

(14) Infidelity: Infidelity can breed lack of trust, create emotional pain and lead to the end of the relationship. It is emotionally devastating for the betrayed partner and can have long-lasting effects on the health of the relationship.

(15) Communication gap: It refers to a lack of effective communication between partners. It results in misunderstandings, misinterpretations, and a breakdown in emotional intimacy and trust.

(16) Not making time for each other: It leads to a lack of emotional connection and intimacy. When partners prioritize other commitments over their relationship, it can create feelings of neglect and resentment which is a recipe for a botched relationship.

(17) Trouble in physical relationship: Difficulty making a physical relationship work in a relationship, such as differences in sexual desire or preferences, physical limitations, or emotional barriers, create tension and frustration between partners.

(18)   Whining all the time: When one partner constantly complains or expresses dissatisfaction, it can create a negative atmosphere that can be draining and stressful for both partners. It is detrimental to the emotional connection between partners.

(19) Unnecessarily being critical: When one partner is constantly critical of the other, it can erode self-esteem and create feelings of inadequacy and frustration. It can create tension and emotional distance between partners.

(20)   Being unromantic: When partners don't prioritize romance or make an effort to show love and affection, it can create a sense of distance and disconnection.

(21) Envy and jealousy: When one partner feels threatened by the other's relationships or accomplishments, it leads to feelings of resentment and mistrust, and create a toxic and unhealthy dynamic between partners.

(22) Your unending insecurities: When one partner is constantly plagued by insecurities, it can lead to a lack of trust and create a negative atmosphere in the relationship, and create tension and emotional distance between partners. As much as you can have insecurities, it's up to you to not allow it to destroy your relationship.

(23) Lack of self-love: When one partner struggles with self-love, it can create emotional distance and lead to feelings of insecurity and inadequacy.

(24) Unspoken expectations: When expectations are not clearly communicated, it can create a sense of confusion and frustration, lead to misunderstandings and disappointment between partners which can damage the relationship.

(25) Dishonesty: Whether it's lying about small things or keeping big secrets, dishonesty can be damaging to emotional intimacy, create a negative atmosphere in the relationship, and erode trust and create a sense of betrayal between partners.

(26) Selfishness: Selfishness in a relationship can create tension and emotional distance between partners. When one partner is overly focused on their own needs and desires, it can lead to neglect of the other partner's needs, which can be damaging to emotional intimacy and the overall health of the relationship.

(27) Lack of interest in your partner: When one partner is not interested in their partner's life or experiences, it creates feelings of loneliness and emotional distance in the other partner, and disconnection in the relationship.

18. RED FLAGS IN RELATIONSHIP

"God will always bring the right people into your life, but you have to let the wrong people walk away." – Joel Osteen

Red flags are signs that insinuate that compatibility is not at the forefront early on, and that truth could have been buried, inherently, deep down. When red flags occur, you are usually aware of them, but choose to ignore them in favor of continuing the relationship. Because you so badly want the relationship to last, you look at it through your rose-tinted glasses, meaning you only see your partner's good points and never their flaws. Deep down, you are probably aware of the problems, and it's important to listen to your intuition when it is sending you a warning. While you constantly give them the benefit of the doubt, but at some point, a red flag should not be ignored. Following are some red flags you shouldn't ignore because it can breed self-doubt, insecurities and domestic violence.

- **Disrespect of boundaries:** Disrespect of boundaries is a sign of deeper issues related to respect, trust, and communication. Boundaries are a crucial component of any healthy relationship, and they help to establish expectations and guidelines for how partners treat each other. When one partner consistently disregards or violates the other's boundaries, it can erode trust and make it difficult for both partners to feel safe and secure in the relationship. If you are experiencing disrespect of boundaries in a relationship, it is important to take action to address the issue, setting clearer boundaries, communicating your needs and expectations more assertively.

- **Excessive control**: Excessive control is a sign of deeper issues related to power, trust, and respect. Excessive control can manifest in different ways. For example, a partner may try to control the other's behavior, decisions, or appearance. They may limit the other's access to friends or family, monitor their activities, or use threats or intimidation to maintain control. Excessive control can be damaging to both partners, as it can create a power imbalance in the relationship and make it difficult for the controlled partner to feel autonomous and independent. It can also lead to feelings of fear, anxiety, and distrust, and can make it difficult for both partners to establish and maintain healthy boundaries. It is important to remember that no one deserves to be controlled or manipulated in a relationship, and seeking help is a sign of strength, not weakness.

- **The relationship feels unequal**: Feeling like the relationship is unequal lead to feelings of resentment, frustration, and anger in the other partner, and can create a sense of imbalance and unfairness in the relationship. For example, one partner may consistently prioritize their needs and desires over the other's, or may use manipulative tactics to maintain power and control in the relationship. Feeling like the relationship is unequal can be damaging to both partners, as it can erode trust, respect, and intimacy. It creates a power imbalance in the relationship, with one partner consistently taking the lead and the other feeling powerless or unheard.

- **Negative words said about you to others:** it's incredibly hurtful and damaging to your self-esteem, and can erode trust and intimacy in the relationship. For example, a partner may spread rumors or gossip about you, criticize you to friends or family members, or use social media to publicly shame or belittle you. It can be damaging to both partners, as it can lead to feelings of betrayal, anger, and resentment. It can also make it difficult to establish and maintain healthy boundaries, as you may feel like your privacy and personal life are being violated.

- **You don't feel heard**: Feeling unheard can occur as your partner dismissing your concerns, interrupting you when you speak, or ignoring your requests or boundaries which can lead to feelings of frustration, anger, and resentment, and can create a sense of distance and disconnection in the relationship. It is important to take actions when this keeps happening by actively listening to your partner and working to understand their perspective, even if you disagree with it.

- **Fear of arousing certain feelings in your partner**: Do you experience fear of angering or upsetting your partner? This is a red flag that shouldn't be ignored as it can lead to feelings of anxiety, guilt, and shame, and can create a sense of emotional isolation and disconnection in the relationship. Addressing this issue may involve working with your partner to establish a culture of emotional safety and trust, where both partners feel comfortable expressing their feelings and needs.

- **Screaming matches**: Screaming matches are not a healthy way to communicate and can be a red flag that there are deeper issues in the relationship. It is important to address these issues before they escalate into something more serious. When people start screaming at each other, it often means that they have lost the ability to communicate effectively. Screaming can be a sign of frustration and anger, and it can make it difficult to have a productive conversation. It is disrespectful and can be a sign of a deeper issue in the relationship. If one person is regularly screaming at the other, it could be a sign that they do not value the other person's feelings or opinions. In some cases, screaming matches can be a form of emotional abuse that one person is using screaming as a way to control or manipulate the other person. It can also be a precursor to physical violence. If a person feels threatened or unsafe during a screaming match, it is important to take that seriously and take steps to protect themselves.

- **Unhappiness and discomfort around your partner:** It a sign of unhealthy dynamics in the relationship including issues with trust, control, or emotional abuse. It is important to reflect on the reasons behind these feelings and to communicate with your partner about how you are feeling. It could be that you are not emotionally connected. This lack of connection could make it difficult to feel fulfilled and satisfied in the relationship. It could also be a breakdown in communication. If you are not able to express your feelings and needs to your partner, it can lead to frustration and resentment. In some cases, feeling unhappy or uncomfortable around your partner could be a sign that you are not compatible. It is important to consider whether your values, goals, and lifestyles align and whether you are truly a good fit for each other.

19. SIGNS OF FALLING OUT OF LOVE

"When love goes bad nothing goes worse."

— *Christopher Hitchens*

Do you no longer feel the spark that was there before, rather the mere presence of your partner annoy you? Falling out of love usually means your relationship is lacking intimacy. People usually fall out of love if one partner isn't willing to grow along with the other partner. Communication issues and unrealistic expectations are two of the main reasons people find themselves falling out of love. It's hard to define exactly what falling out of love feels like, but it's usually characterized by actions (or lack thereof) that detract from intimacy in a relationship. These are some signs that you have fallen out of love or are currently falling out of love with your partner?

- You're no longer excited to spend time together

- You're not open with your partner

- You seek out opportunities to avoid your partner

- You feel uncertain about your future with them

- You're longing for someone (or something) else

- You're overly defensive

- You constantly criticize your partner

- You're thinking about them less and less.

- They start to feel like a burden.

- Their behavior is increasingly annoying to you.

- You're no longer having meaningful conversations.

- You're no longer fighting.

- You have more negative thoughts than positive thoughts.

- At least one person seems distant and unhappy

- You don't worry about them as much.

- You're no longer proud to be with them.

- Physical intimacy is a thing of the past.

- You don't plan dates..

- You no longer prioritize them.

- You start complaining about them…to everyone.

- They don't feel special to you.

- You're less interested in spending time with them.

When the interests that once brought a couple together start to diverge, it's normal to feel a lack of connection. It's also helpful for couples of any stage of their relationship to put effort into making sure their lives have enough novelty, variety, and surprise.

20. SIGNS OF A TOXIC RELATIONSHIP

"There are people who bring you down, by just being them"

– Malebo Sephodi

When you first meet someone, the world is a beautiful place. The trees are greener, the candy is sweeter and everything is just, well, great. But as the honeymoon period fizzles out, masks begin to slip and reveal a much uglier truth. You find yourself trapped, unappreciated and unloved by the person you've given so much energy and time to. Evidently, not everyone wants the best for you. Not everyone wants you to shine, to be happy, and successful. Some people even enjoy your misery and despair, feeding the doubts whilst driving you down a powerless spiral of torment. The caring turns to control and the togetherness becomes a toxic prison. The bitterness weighs us down, and every day feels like groundhog day. It can be hard to see a way out. The main goal of a toxic person is to reduce the way you see yourself drastically and increase themselves. A toxic person will do all they can to intimidate you and the best step to take if you notice these steps is to leave that relationship immediately. Following are signs for a toxic relationship.

1) Lack of support: When one partner feels unsupported, it can lead to feelings of resentment, disconnection, and even the breakdown of the relationship. Lack of support from your partner shows you exactly what you should know --they don't care about you.

2) Diminished self-worth: If you feel your self-worth and self-love gradually declining with every word your partner says or actions barbed at you, that relationship is toxic.

3) Name-calling: When your partner starts calling you insulting and snarky names, either in front of people or when you are alone, that relationship has long turned toxic. Nobody should call their partners snarky names, not even teasing. As long as boundaries are established rightly, once your boundary is being crossed repeatedly with no regard to your feeling, your relationship is toxic.

4) Toxic communication: A sign of toxicity is when your conversations have gotten sarcastic, snarky and impolite with no regards to your feelings.

5) Envy or jealousy: When your partner starts getting envious and jealous at every move you or someone else makes, that relationship is on the fast track to being a controlling relationship. Envy or jealousy should not exist in a trust filled relationship and it mostly likely happens because of insecurities in the toxic partner.

6) Gaslighting: Gaslighting is a form of psychological manipulation in which the abuser attempts to sow self-doubt and confusion in their victim's mind. Typically, gas lighters are seeking to gain power and control over the other person, by distorting reality and forcing them to question their own judgment and intuition. Gaslighting is not easily noticed, and a toxic person can easily manipulate their partners by gaslighting them. These are some signs of gaslighting in a relationship:

- Lying about or denying something and refusing to admit the lie even when you show them proof;

- Insisting that an event or behavior you witnessed never happened and that you're remembering it wrong;

- Spreading rumors and gossip about you, or telling you that other people are gossiping about you;

- Changing the subject or refusing to listen when confronted about a lie or other gaslighting behavior;

- Telling you that you're overreacting when you call them out;

- Blame shifting in relationships—saying that if you acted differently, they wouldn't treat you like this, so it's your fault;

- Trying to smooth things over with loving words that don't match their actions;

- Twisting a story to minimize their abusive behavior;

- Minimizing their hurtful behaviors or words by saying, "It was just a joke" or "You're way too sensitive";

- Separating you from friends and family who might recognize the gaslighting abuse symptoms.

7) Threats of self-harm: Threats of self-harm is another effective way that abusers manipulate their victims. The truth is that sometimes, they are not bluffing but most times, they are.

8)Physical violence: It should not get to this before you start seeing the signs of danger and if you are indeed at this point, nothing your partner is saying is right.

8) Controlling behaviors: Your partner has gotten extremely controlling towards you. They are controlling what you wear, what you eat, who you talk to, what social gathering, if any, you attend. This is not a sign of love. It's okay for your partner to have preferences on you but they should not bond their preferences on you.

9) Patterns of disrespect: When your partner starts treating you with disrespect, the relationship is toxic and it's left for you to state your boundary.

10) Resentment: Resentment is a feeling of anger or bitterness that arises from a sense of unfairness or mistreatment. It can often develop in relationships where one partner feels that their needs or wants are consistently overlooked or dismissed by the other partner. Some causes of resentment are: unmet needs, lack of communication, power imbalances. Resentment can also come as a result of falling out of love with your partner so it's best to examine the source of the resentment you feel before labelling your relationship toxic.

11) Financial restrictions: There is a difference between restrictions based on love or because you both don't make much and your expenses is eating up a bulk of what it is but if the financial restriction is as a result of having one more sector in your life being controlled, the relationship is most definitely toxic.

12) Constant stress: Are you constantly crying? Constantly feeling depressed or stressed out? As long as your tears and stress is from your relationship, the relationship is not healthy for you. Your level of happiness should outweigh your level of unhappiness.

13) Ignoring your needs: Does your partner ignore your needs? Does your partner always expect you to put your needs and wants on the back burner when it concerns them?

14) Lost relationships: Is your partner constantly encouraging you to hang out with only them all the time? Is your partner not allowing you to see your friends or family? A healthy relationship seeks for you to maintain your relationships with friends and families as well as with them. Lost relationships can come from different reasons so make sure to dig deep to know why you seem to be losing or have lost your relationships. Loss of past relationship doesn't only stem from toxic partners, it can also be wholly your fault.

15) Lack of self-care: In a toxic relationship, one or both partners may neglect their own self-care. This can happen for a variety of reasons, such as feeling like they don't have the time or energy to focus on themselves, or because the toxic dynamics of the relationship have left them feeling drained and depleted. If you are in a toxic relationship and find yourself neglecting self-care, it's important to take steps to prioritize your well-being. This might mean setting boundaries with your partner, seeking support from friends, and engaging in activities that bring you joy and relaxation.

16) Always walking on eggshells: If you feel like you have to be constantly careful about what you say or do to avoid triggering your partner's anger, it may be a sign that your relationship is emotionally abusive. In a healthy relationship, partners should be able to communicate openly and honestly without fear of retaliation or punishment. They should also be able to express their feelings and opinions without being criticized or belittled.

17) Secrecy and fear: Secrecy and fear are common in toxic relationships, and they can be extremely damaging to both parties involved. In a toxic relationship, one or both partners may feel the need to keep secrets or hide certain aspects of themselves out of fear of the other person's reaction. This can lead to a cycle of mistrust and suspicion, where both partners are constantly questioning each other's motives and actions. It can also create an environment of fear and anxiety, where one partner is afraid of how the other person will react if they reveal their true thoughts or feelings. In some cases, secrecy and fear may be used as a form of control or manipulation by one partner. They may use threats or intimidation to keep the other person in line, or they may use secrecy as a way to keep the other person isolated and dependent on them.

18) Emotional disconnect: Emotional disconnect can occur when one or both partners start to shut down emotionally and distance themselves from the relationship. This occurs when one or both partners are unable and unwilling to connect with each other. This can happen for a variety of reasons, including feelings of resentment, betrayal, or neglect.

19) Lack of intimacy: Lack of intimacy in a relationship can be a common issue, as toxic behaviors such as manipulation, control, and emotional abuse can make it difficult for partners to feel safe and connected with each other. Intimacy include physical closeness, as well as emotional and psychological closeness as well. In a toxic relationship, intimacy may be lacking in all of these areas, leaving both partners feeling disconnected and alone. For example, a partner who is emotionally abusive may use tactics such as gaslighting, belittling, and blaming to control and manipulate their partner, which can make it difficult for the partner to feel emotionally close or safe. Alternatively, a partner who is overly critical or controlling may make it difficult for their partner to feel comfortable and relaxed during physical intimacy, leading to a lack of physical intimacy.

20) Lack of commitment: In a toxic relationship, lack of commitment can manifest in different ways. For example, a partner may avoid making plans for the future or refuse to discuss the relationship's status, leaving the other partner feeling uncertain about the future. Lack of commitment in a toxic relationship can be damaging to both partners, as it can prevent them from feeling secure and connected with each other. It is important to recognize that lack of commitment in a toxic relationship is not solely the responsibility of one partner. Both partners may contribute to the toxicity of the relationship, and both may need to take steps to address their behaviors and rebuild trust if they want to salvage the relationship. Seeking support from a therapist or counselor can be helpful in navigating this process.

21. HOW TO LEAVE A TOXIC RELATIONSHIP

"A bad relationship can make you doubt everything good you ever felt about yourself." – Dionne Warwick

A healthy relationship maked you feel good. A toxic relationship keeps dragging you down. It never helps you in becoming better while a healthy one does. Like arsenic, toxic people will slowly kill you. They kill your positive spirit and play with your mind and emotions. The only cure is to let them go. You cannot thrive in toxic relationships. Let them go so you can grow. Until you let go of all the toxic people in your life, you will never be able to grow into your fullest potential.

Relationships are NOT supposed to make you feel bad, or guilty, insecure, ashamed, paranoid, or hopeless. So when a relationship makes you feel bad, guilty, insecure, ashamed, paranoid, or hopeless, end it.

A bad relationship is like standing on broken glass, if you stay you will keep hurting. If you walk away, you will hurt but eventually you will heal. Ending an unhealthy relationship is not only courageous, but a monumental step in working towards a healthier relationship with yourself and others. Leaving a toxic relationship is never easy no matter how toxic it was because the relationship was an entire betrayal of the trust you once had in that person. You have to realize that you are not alone and you didn't do anything shameful. You are doing the right thing for yourself by leaving regardless of when you really got the courage to.

• Get support from a therapist or domestic violence advocate: You are not alone, even if you feel like you no longer have friends or families that will be there for you, remember that you are not the only one that have gone through that journey.

• Open up to loved ones; You have to open up to your loved ones about what you are going through. They are the best set of people to have with you when leaving.

• Take good care of yourself: This is extremely important. It's very easy for you to wallow in pity and despair. You have to take care of yourself. Give yourself an achievement goal, "It's been 6 months before I escaped that relationship, I want to see something change in me". It keeps you going forward and helps a big deal when improving your self-worth.

22. WHEN THE RELATIONSHIP ISN'T GOING WELL?

"We have to recognize that there cannot be relationships unless there is commitment, unless there is loyalty, unless there is love, patience, persistence." – Cornel West

If you are unhappy in your relationship, you need to identify the issues that are bothering you, discuss them with your partner, and work together to find solutions. You might be going through some of the rough patches we may have mentioned in the different sections and maybe you're wondering if your relationship is still worth saving or if it's finally over. Don't break up, fix the problem. Start the romance again. Go on dates again. Work on winning each other over again. Here are some things you can do to try to bring back your relationship to where it was as long as you're both ready to fight for your relationship.

1)   **Shift from blaming to understanding**: It is a powerful tool for improving communication and resolving conflicts in any type of relationship. Blaming someone can be a defensive tactic that shuts down communication. When you shift to understanding, you can

create an atmosphere of open communication where both parties feel heard and valued. Understanding someone else's perspective can increase your empathy for them. When you try to see things from their point of view, you may be more likely to find common ground and work towards a resolution that works for both of you. Blaming someone can put them on the defensive, which can make it more difficult to find a solution. When you shift to understanding, you can create a less adversarial atmosphere where both parties can work together towards a common goal. Shifting from blaming to understanding can help you to identify the root causes of a conflict and work towards a resolution that addresses those underlying issues. This can lead to more effective problem-solving and a stronger, more productive relationship. Overall, shifting from blaming to understanding can be a powerful way to improve communication, increase empathy, reduce defensiveness, and resolve conflicts in any type of relationship.

2) **Willingness to invest:** Willingness to invest in a relationship is an important factor in building and maintaining strong, healthy relationships. It requires a commitment to making the relationship work, a willingness to communicate openly and honestly, and a

desire to build intimacy and emotional connection with your partner. Being willing to invest time, energy, and resources into a relationship shows a commitment to making it work. This commitment can help to build trust and strengthen the bond between two people. Investing in a relationship can help to build intimacy and emotional connection. When you make an effort to understand your partner, spend time with them, and share experiences, you can deepen your relationship and create a stronger bond. Investing in a relationship requires good communication skills. When you are willing to listen, express your feelings, and work through conflicts, you can create a more open and honest dialogue with your partner. When both partners are willing to invest in a relationship, it can create a sense of security and stability. This can help to reduce anxiety and uncertainty and create a more positive, supportive relationship environment.

3) **Openness to seek outside help**: Openness to seek outside help in a relationship is a sign of strength and a willingness to work towards a healthy, strong partnership. It can provide a fresh perspective, help break patterns of behavior, and improve communication skills, ultimately leading to a stronger, more positive relationship. It demonstrates a commitment to making the

relationship work. It shows that you are willing to put in the time and effort necessary to build a healthy, strong partnership. Seeking outside help can provide a fresh perspective and help both partners gain new insights into the issues they are facing. If a relationship is stuck in unhealthy patterns of behavior, seeking outside help can help break those patterns and create new, healthier ones. This can be especially important if the partners are struggling to communicate effectively or are repeating the same arguments over and over again. Working with a trained professional can help improve communication skills in a relationship. This can include learning how to express emotions effectively, active listening, and conflict resolution techniques.

4) **Don't dwell on the past**: This means that both partners are willing to move forward and focus on the present and future instead of dwelling on past mistakes or grievances. To build a healthy relationship, you have to be willing to let go of the past. This can be challenging, as everyone brings their own history and experiences into a relationship, but it is crucial for building a healthy and strong partnership. Remember, letting go of the past doesn't mean forgetting about it entirely. It simply means acknowledging it, learning from it,

and using it as a foundation for a stronger and more fulfilling future together.

5) **View your partner with compassion**: It means that you see them not just as a partner, but as a human being with their own struggles, fears, and insecurities. It involves approaching your relationship with kindness, understanding, and empathy, even in difficult times. Here are some tips for viewing your partner with compassion in a relationship:

- Practice empathy: Try to put yourself in your partner's shoes and understand their perspective. Listen to them without judgment and try to see things from their point of view.

- Show kindness: Show your partner kindness in both big and small ways. This could mean doing something thoughtful for them, expressing gratitude for the things they do, or simply being patient and understanding when they're having a hard day.

- Be supportive: Support your partner through both their triumphs and their struggles. Be their cheerleader and help them through difficult times.

- Practice forgiveness: No one is perfect, and everyone makes mistakes. Practice forgiveness and let go of grudges or resentment.

- Communicate openly: Communicate openly and honestly with your partner, and encourage them to do the same. This will help you both to understand each other's needs and feelings better.

- Be patient: Remember that change takes time, and be patient with your partner as they grow and work through their own issues.

6) Be accountable: Accountability in a relationship means taking responsibility for your actions and holding yourself and your partner accountable for maintaining the trust, respect, and integrity of the relationship. It involves being honest, open, and willing to take ownership of your mistakes and work towards solutions. Here are some ways in which accountability can be fostered in a relationship:

- Communication: Open and honest communication is key to building trust and fostering accountability in a relationship. Both partners should feel comfortable sharing their thoughts, feelings, and concerns, and be willing to listen and respond with empathy.

- Respect: Respecting each other's boundaries and opinions is essential for a healthy and accountable relationship. It means acknowledging and honoring other's perspectives, even when you don't agree.

- Responsibility: Each partner should take responsibility for their actions and decisions, and should be willing to own up to any mistakes or missteps. This involves being accountable for the impact that your behavior has on the relationship, and being willing to make amends when necessary.

- Trust: Trust is built through consistent, reliable, and accountable behavior. Each partner should demonstrate their trustworthiness by following through on commitments, being honest and transparent, and taking responsibility for their actions.

7) **Heal individually:** It can allow each partner to be more present and engaged in the relationship, communicate more effectively, better understand and empathize with each other's needs and perspectives, thus lead to a healthier and more fulfilling relationship. Both individuals have their own unique experiences, histories, and emotions that can impact the relationship. Individual healing can involve working through past traumas, addressing personal issues, and developing coping mechanisms to deal with stress or anxiety. This can include seeking therapy or counseling, practicing self-care, engaging in activities that bring joy and fulfillment, and taking time for introspection and reflection.

23. HOW TO MAINTAIN A HEALTHY AND HAPPY RELATIONSHIP

"If you want a relationship that looks and feels like the most amazing thing on earth, you need to treat it like it's the most amazing thing on earth"–Your tango.

Maintaining a healthy and happy relationship is not rocket science neither is it very easy. It only comes by deliberate steps and strategies together. Both partners have to intentionally do all they can to maintain their relationship. Not that there will not be conflicts but conflicts are resolved amicably. Even though each relationship is different, there are basic tips and guidelines to follow to keep it healthy and happy.

1) **Embrace each other's differences:** Embracing each other's differences in a relationship can be a key factor in building a strong and healthy connection. Every individual has their own unique personality, beliefs, values, and experiences that shape who they are. These differences can enrich the relationship and create opportunities for personal growth and learning.

2) Consider their perspectives: Considering your partner's perspective in your relationship is important to build empathy and understanding. When you take the time to see things from your partner's point of view, you can better understand their thoughts, feelings, and actions, which can lead to more effective communication and a stronger relationship.

3) Solve problems together: Solving problems together is important to build trust, respect, and a deeper connection with your partner. When you work through challenges as a team, you can develop effective communication skills, improve your problem-solving abilities, and strengthen your bond as a couple.

4) Talk about your goals and dreams: Sharing your hopes and aspirations can help you to understand each other's values, priorities, and motivations, and to create a vision for your future together. It is powerful way to deepen your connection with your partner and build a shared sense of purpose.

5) Keep your expectations realistic: Keeping your expectations realistic in your relationship is important to avoid disappointment, resentment, and misunderstandings. Unrealistic expectations can create unnecessary pressure and tension, and can be a major source of conflict in relationships. This can be achieved through open and clear communication, focusing on what is important, being able and willing to compromise, e.t.c.

6) **Talk with each other**: Talking with each other is essential for building a strong and healthy connection. Communication is the foundation of any relationship, and it is important to establish a habit of open, honest, and respectful communication with your partner.

7) **Be dependable**: Being dependable is important to build trust, respect, and a strong foundation for your connection with your partner. Dependability means following through on your commitments, being reliable, and showing up for your partner when they need you.

8) **Fight fair**: Fighting fair is important to resolve conflicts in a healthy and productive way. Disagreements are a natural part of any relationship, but it's important to handle them in a way that respects your partner and maintains the integrity of your connection.

9) **Keep your life balanced**: Keeping your life balanced is important to maintain your overall well-being and to avoid becoming overly dependent on your partner. A balanced life can help you to

maintain your sense of identity, pursue your interests and goals, and remain emotionally and mentally healthy.

10) It's a process: Your relationship is a process that involves continuous growth and development. Relationships require effort, commitment, and willingness to adapt to changes over time. It's important to understand that a relationship is not a static entity and that it will evolve as you and your partner grow and change.

11) Be yourself: Being yourself in your relationship is essential to building a strong and healthy connection with your partner. Being authentic and true to yourself can help you to establish a deeper level of intimacy and trust with your partner, and it can also help you to maintain a sense of personal fulfillment and happiness.

12) Try not to focus on trifles: Trying not to focus on trifles in your relationship is important to maintain a positive and harmonious connection with your partner. Trifles refer to small and insignificant issues that may not have any significant impact on your relationship, but can still cause unnecessary stress and tension.

13) Focus on the positive: Always focusing on the positive in your relationship is important to maintain a healthy and fulfilling connection with your partner. Positive emotions and experiences can help to strengthen your bond, increase your sense of satisfaction and happiness, and improve overall relationship quality.

14) **Let your words carry your actions**: it's not just about what you say, but also about how you act. Your actions can often speak louder than words and have a significant impact on the success of your relationship.

24. SUCCESSFUL DATING FOR MARRIAGE

"I would rather share one lifetime with you, than face all the ages of this world alone."

—J.R.R. Tolkien

When you meet someone purely for the hunt of a partner, it's called dating for marriage. On the surface, dating for marriage doesn't look much different from dating in general. You'll still go out to dinner with someone, maybe see a movie or have a picnic in the park. The two main differences are that you'll only do these things with someone you're genuinely interested in pursuing. And you'll talk about deeper topics on the date to determine whether or not there is potential for a long-term relationship.

Marriage is the process by which two people make their relationship public, official, and permanent. Successful dating will eventually lead to marriage. However, finding a partner for marriage takes time, effort, and patience. Know with all certainty that marriage is a lifelong commitment, and it should be taken seriously.

When you are dating the goal of establishing a healthy marriage, it is very important to pick partners who have similar relationship goals who are also are dating for the purposes of finding someone to marry. Both you and your spouse need to be on the same page and share the same interests in order to make the relationship last.

Finding the right partner takes time, so be patient and don't rush into anything. Rushing into a relationship rarely ends well. Take the time to get to know the person and build a solid foundation for your relationship. Remember, it's better to wait for the right person than to settle for someone who is not right for you. Take your time, be honest and authentic, communicate effectively, and be respectful and patient.

Most couples date for two or more years before getting engaged, with many dating anywhere from two to five years. Once the question is popped, the average length of engagement is between 12 and 18 months. The average length of a relationship before marriage is between two and five years. For people who are over 40, it is better to date for no more than six months before making a decision. During the first three months of dating, you should be building your exclusivity as a couple. It's imperative that you're very clear from the beginning that you're a marriage-minded person (if you are) and that your partner is on the same path as you. By the time you've reached the six-month mark, you should be prepared for engagement, unless there are extenuating circumstances, or you may have to break off the relationship if you are not both on the same page with respect to timing. Yes, for those in search of lasting love, their time is precious and matters.

Further, about half of survey respondents said couples who live together before marriage have a better chance of having a successful marriage than those who don't. Once a couple does decide to get married, though, it tends to lead to higher rates of satisfaction than just living together.

Marriage does more than change people's living situation and daily routines. The choice of spouse is among the most important decisions most people ever make. The science of relationships offers some insights into how successful partners tend to find each other, but whether or not a marriage will last ultimately depends on the specific characteristics of the individuals deciding to unite.

REFERENCES

1. loveisrespect.org

2. https://www.independent.co.uk/life-style/love-sex/toxic-healthy-relationship-partner-signs-b2203440.html

3. https://www.ny.gov/teen-dating-violence-awareness-and-prevention/what-does-healthy-relationship-look#:~:text=Healthy%20relationships%20involve%20honesty%2C%20trust,or%20retaliation%2C%20and%20share%20decisions.

4. https://theeverygirl.com/new-relationship-advice/

5. https://www.waldenu.edu/programs/psychology/resource/ten-signs-of-a-healthy-relationship

6. https://eugenetherapy.com/article/5-signs-of-a-healthy-relationship/

7. https://www.jordanharbinger.com/8-signs-your-relationship-isnt-working-and-whether-you-should-break-up-or-fix-it/

8. https://www.healthline.com/health/toxic-relationship#signs-of-toxicity

9. https://www.brides.com/falling-out-love-4150474#:~:text=Besides%20no%20longer%20getting%20excited,longer%20than%20you%20have%20to.

10. https://www.brides.com/falling-out-love-4150474#:~:text=Besides%20no%20longer%20getting%20excited,longer%20than%20you%20have%20to

11. https://www.healthline.com/health/toxic-relationship#can-it-be-fixed

12. https://www.lifehack.org/articles/communication/10-ways-spend-more-quality-time-with-your-partner.html

13. https://www.healthline.com/health/toxic-relationship#leaving-a-toxic-relationship

14. https://www.jordanharbinger.com/8-signs-your-relationship-isnt-working-and-whether-you-should-break-up-or-fix-it/

15. https://www.marriage.com/advice/relationship/ways-to-have-a-quality-time-with-your-partner/

16. https://www.lifehack.org/358731/11-tips-that-help-couples-keep-growing-relationship

17. https://www.marriage.com/advice/relationship/affection-in-a-relationship/

18. https://www.entrepreneur.com/leadership/7-steps-to-compromising-effectively-as-a-business-leader/296637

19. https://www.lifehack.org/articles/communication/7-ways-learning-compromise-improves-all-your-relationships.html

20. https://simipsychologicalgroup.com/how-to-boost-your-partners-confidence/

21. https://goodmenproject.com/featured-content/how-to-boost-your-partners-self-esteem-with-these-6-actions/

22. https://www.marriage.com/advice/relationship/tips-to-maintain-commitment-in-your-relationship/

23. https://www.lovepanky.com/love-couch/better-love/how-to-show-commitment-in-a-relationship

24. https://www.keen.com/articles/love/6-tips-to-keep-the-commitment-in-your-relationship

25. https://www.healthline.com/health/healthy-relationship#tips

26. https://counselorforcouples.com/why-kindness-is-important-perhaps-the-most-important-quality/

27. https://www.womenshealthmag.com/relationships/a29212428/when-you-find-the-one/

28. https://www.fashionbeans.com/content/how-you-know-youve-found-the-one/

29. https://familiesforlife.sg/discover-an-article/Pages/8-Signs-that-Say-You've-Found-The-One.aspx

30. https://psychcentral.com/health/why-men-give-up-their-identity-in-a-relationship#4-tips-to-maintain-identity

31. https://www.weddingwire.com/wedding-ideas/losing-individuality

32. https://www.mayoclinichealthsystem.org/hometown-health/speaking-of-health/7-anger-management-tips-to-prevent-relationship-damage

33. https://www.wikihow.com/Control-Anger-in-a-Relationship

34. https://www.psycom.net/control-anger-frustration-relationship

35. https://www.marriage.com/advice/relationship/managing-anger-in-relationship/

36. https://www.self.com/story/fighting-fair

37. https://www.foryourmarriage.org/25-ways-to-fight-fair/

38. https://www.marriage.com/advice/relationship/tips-for-fighting-fair-in-relationship/

39. https://www.heysigmund.com/fighting-fair/

40. https://www.symbis.com/blog/8-ways-to-make-a-strong-decision-together/

41. https://www.tonyrobbins.com/love-relationships/your-decision-my-decision-our-decision/

42. https://www.skillsyouneed.com/ips/joint-decision-making.html

43. https://www.marriage.com/advice/relationship/ways-to-make-a-strong-decision-together/

44. https://www.fatherly.com/life/how-to-make-better-joint-decisions

45. https://www.gottman.com/blog/managing-conflict-solvable-vs-perpetual-problems/

46. https://www.therapyroute.com/article/managing-perpetual-conflicts-in-marriage-by-p-kuruga

47. https://www.sdicouples.com/sdicblog/2022/1/22/a-relationship-with-shared-meaning

48. https://www.gottman.com/blog/shared-meaning-is-key-to-a-successful-relationship/

49. https://www.jordanharbinger.com/8-signs-your-relationship-isnt-working-and-whether-you-should-break-up-or-fix-it/

50. https://www.happywedding.app/blog/things-that-can-destroy-your-relationships/

51. https://bestlifeonline.com/relationship-quotes/#:~:text=%22Love%20is%20composed%20of%20a%20single%20soul%20inhabiting%20two%20bodies.%22&text=%22I%20would%20rather%20share%20one,ages%20of%20this%20world%20alone.%22&text=%22The%20best%20thing%20to%20hold,in%20life%20is%20each%20other.%22&text=%22You%20know%20you're%20in,finally%20better%20than%20your%20dreams.%22

52. https://www.mindbodygreen.com/articles/clear-signs-youre-falling-out-of-love-according-to-experts

53. https://www.womansday.com/relationships/dating-marriage/g27321468/falling-out-of-love-signs/

54. https://parade.com/1153715/marynliles/falling-out-of-love-signs/

ABOUT THE AUTHOR

 Susan Su holds a Ph.D. from U. C. Berkeley in engineering. She worked in the National Berkeley National Lab, consulted for National Aeronautics and Space Administration (NASA). She published many scientific papers at international and national journals. She is also a prolific author of fictions, non-fictions and screenplays.

SUSAN SU © 2023

Printed by Libri Plureos GmbH in Hamburg,
Germany